HOW TO WATCH
AMERICAN FOOTBALL

HOW TO WATCH
AMERICAN FOOTBALL

John L. Johnston

Illustrations based on photographs
by Cliff Brown

TARGET

A TARGET BOOK
published by
the Paperback Division of
W. H. ALLEN & Co. PLC

A Target Book
Published in 1984
by the Paperback Division of
W. H. Allen & Co. PLC
44 Hill Street, London W1X 8LB

First published in the U.S.A.
by Tribeca Communications, Inc. 1984
under the title *How to Watch Football*

Printed and bound in Great Britain by
Anchor Brendon Ltd, Tiptree, Essex

ISBN 0 426 20175 2

Special thanks to Jon Calvert
and to the staff of The Bookmakers, Incorporated

CONTENTS

HOW TO WATCH
AMERICAN FOOTBALL

INTRODUCTION

To the untrained eye, American football is a game where two opposing groups of heavily padded men line up, charge at each other to form a tangled mass of bodies, and then limp back to huddle with their teammates. Every so often somebody throws or kicks the ball in the air and whoever catches it gets slammed to the ground. A game of American football looks as subtle as a car crash—and a bit less interesting.

To the student of the game, each play represents the meshing of speed, strength, skill, teamwork, intensity, and hard work. What the novice sees as a 22-man pileup is actually an intricately-designed, coordinated movement of players, the culmination of months of practice and planning. A hard-fought contest is a match of finesse, guts, and strategy.

American football is a complex game. It can be hard to follow and even harder to appreciate without a basic understanding of its rules, techniques, and strategies. This book can help you learn more about the game. *How to Watch American Football* is written to take the mystery out of the tangled masses of bodies and help you learn how each play is a product of design—an offensive action and a defensive counteraction.

A BRIEF DESCRIPTION OF THE RULES

The Field

A football field is 120 yards long and 160 feet wide. At each end is a zone 10 yards deep, called an *end zone*. The distance from one end zone to the other is 100 yards. The striped lines across the field are spaced 5 yards apart and are called *yard markers*. They are numbered by the distance to the nearest end zone. The center is the 50-yard marker; the stripes 5 yards to each side of the 50 mark the 45-yard line. The perimeter of the 120-yard field represents the out-of-bounds line. All play must occur within these lines.

The Clock

Each game is composed of one hour of playing time, which is divided into two halves of 30 minutes each. The time is also divided into four quarters of 15 minutes each.

The Teams

Football is played by two teams. Although teams generally have rosters of forty or more, only eleven players are allowed on the playing field at one time. Players may be substituted for each other between plays, and unlimited substitution is allowed.

The object of the game is to outscore the opponent. Each team defends one end of the field and tries to move the football into the other end zone while defending its own.

Scoring

The primary unit of scoring is the touchdown. If a team has possession of the football in its opponent's end zone, that team scores a touchdown (six points).

If a team placekicks the ball through the goalposts erected behind its opponent's goal line (the ball must go *over* the crossbar and *between* the uprights), that team scores a field goal (three points).

After any touchdown, the team which scored is given one play to go for a conversion from the 2-yard line. In most cases, the offense elects to try a placekick. If the kick is through the goalposts, the team is given one point.

If a team is tackled with the ball in its own end zone, the opposing team is awarded a safety (two points).

Moving the Ball

The basic unit of a football field is the yard. In order to score, teams try to move the football across the yard markers and toward their opponent's end zone. Each play starts at a particular yard line on the field, which is called the *line of scrimmage*. The team can move the ball by running with it until they are tackled or go out of bounds—the place where the ball carrier was tackled or was last in bounds becomes the new line of scrimmage.

The team can also choose to pass the ball, throwing it in the air to a teammate. If the teammate catches the ball in bounds, he can then run with the ball, and the new line of scrimmage will be wherever he is tackled or goes out-of-bounds. If the ball is not caught before it touches the ground, it is considered an *incomplete pass*. On an incomplete pass there is no gain or loss of yardage, and the ball is put back on the original line of scrimmage.

While the team with possession of the ball (the *offensive team*) is trying to advance the ball, the team without the ball (the *defense*) is doing its best to keep them from gaining yards. On running plays the defense tries to tackle the man with the ball (grab him so that his knees touch the ground). When the ball is passed, the defenders try to knock it to the ground before it is caught or else to catch the football themselves.

First Downs

When a team gains possession of the ball, it is given four *downs* (chances to put the ball in play) to move the ball 10 yards. If they can move the ball 10 yards, then they gain another first down and will again have four plays to move the next 10 yards. On virtually every play of the game, the primary goal of the offense will be to reach the next *first down*. If a first down play gains 6 yards, then the offense's position will be *second and four*—second down with 4 yards to go for the first down.

Technically, a team has four plays to get the 10 yards needed for a new first down. In fact, a team will rarely use more then three. If a team does not have the first down after three tries, they will use the fourth to kick the ball. If they are close enough to the goal posts, they will try a field goal. Otherwise they will *punt* the ball and give the other team the opportunity to go on offense. (See "The Punt", page 8 7.) Just as the goal of the offense is to make first downs, the goal of the defense is to prevent the offense from reaching the first downs, so that they can regain possession of the ball.

Changes of Possession

There are six ways that possesion of the ball can be changed:

1. A team which scores a field goal or a touchdown kicks the ball off to the opponent. After a safety, the team which was trapped must punt the ball off to the team which scored.
2. If the offense fails to gain a first down in four tries, the defense takes over.
3. When a player with possession of the football loses control and fumbles, the team which ends up with control of the ball gets possession.
4. A pass can be intercepted by the defending team.
5. A punt transfers possession to the receiving team.
6. After a missed field goal, the defending team gains possession at the line of scrimmage before the kick.

Whenever there is a change of possession, the team on offense starts with a first down.

Penalties

Despite appearances, not everything is allowed on the football field. Each game is carefully patrolled by a referee, an umpire, a linesman, a line judge, a field judge, a back judge, and a side judge. They monitor the game and dole out penalties when rules are broken. (*See Figure 1.*) A penalty can be in the form of a loss of down, a loss of yardage, or both—most penalties involve a loss of 5, 10, or 15 yards and a repeat of the down. When an official sees a penalty, he will take a yellow cloth out of his back pocket and throw it into the air. If the play is already in progress, it will be allowed to continue to its conclusion. After it is over, the team which is the victim of the penalty will have an opportunity to accept the results of the play or to have the penalty assessed.

The officials also determine when and where each play ends. When the official closest to the play feels the ball carrier has been tackled or the pass has fallen incomplete, he will blow a whistle to signify the end of the play. The official will then make a determination as to where the play ended and *spot the ball*, establishing the new line of scrimmage.

A BRIEF DESCRIPTION OF THE RULES

ROUGHING THE KICKER

ILLEGAL PROCEDURE

DELAY OF GAME

TIME OUT

PASS OR KICK INTERFERENCE

ILLEGAL USE OF HANDS

PERSONAL FOUL

BALL IS DEAD

INCOMPLETE FORWARD PASS

Figure 1. *Officials' signals.*

FIRST DOWN

ILLEGAL MOTION

GAME CLOCK STARTS

OFFSIDE

PERSONAL FOUL

SAFETY

SCORE

Stopping the Clock

When does a sixty-minute game take three hours? When it's football. The game clock does not run continuously while the players are on the field. It is stopped whenever there is a penalty or an incomplete pass, and whenever a player goes out of bounds with the ball, and it doesn't start to run again until the ball is put in motion on the next play. In high school and college, when a team makes a first down the clock is stopped until the referees get the new first down marked. Each team is also given three time outs in each half, which can be used to stop the clock.

A BRIEF DESCRIPTION OF THE RULES

Key to figures

◯   offensive player

▢   defensive player

Ⓧ   split end

Ⓨ   tight end

Ⓩ   flanker

☐S   safety

☐C   cornerback

☐B   linebacker

••••••••••   quarterback motion

- - - - -   ball in the air on pass or lateral

———➤   (for offense) movement of receivers in pass patterns

➤   (for defense) movement of defenders to contain ball carrier

⌐   blocking pattern for offensive player

〰〰   movement of back running with ball or as man in motion

✦✦✦✦✦✦✦✦   movement of defensive backs covering on pass play

- -➤- -➤   kicked ball

THE PLAYERS

Moving the ball up the field against eleven stubborn defensemen takes a well-drilled unit of specialists who represent a variety of skills and talents.

The Offense

The basic offense is composed of five linemen, three receivers, two running backs, and one quarterback. Each team must have seven men on the line of scrimmage, with four at least a yard back from the line. (The quarterback is allowed to be within a yard if he is receiving the ball.) The four backfield players and two *end* positions on the line are eligible to receive a pass or a handoff; the five interior lineman are not. (*See Figure 2.*)

The Defense

The eleven defensive players can be on or off the line as they wish. There are three different units within the defense: linemen, who play right on the line of scrimmage, play the run and rush the quarterback; linebackers, who bridge the responsiblity of stopping runners and covering receivers; and defensive backs, who have the primary responsibility of covering the wide receivers on pass plays. (*See Figure 3.*)

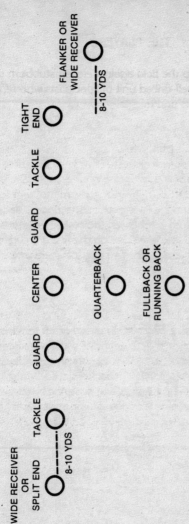

Figure 2. Offensive nomenclature.

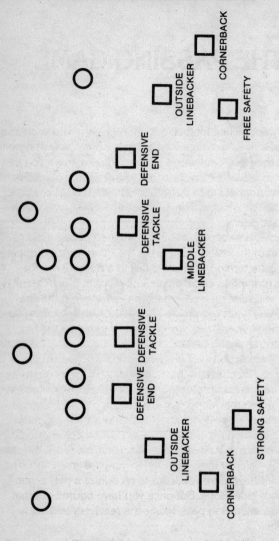

Figure 3. *Defensive nomenclature.*

THE PASSING GAME

To fully appreciate football, you should learn to recognize a play as quickly as possible. The sooner you are able to figure out what the offensive team is trying to do, the more you can evaluate what they are able to do. If you can figure out quickly that the team is going to pass, then you will have more time to follow the pass routes being run by the receivers and watch the play unfold.

To identify a pass play, watch the quarterback and the receivers when the ball is snapped. Is the quarterback dropping back, or is he turning to give the ball to a runner? Are the receivers running to elude the defenders or to block them? Is the tight end running a pass pattern or diving into the linebacker? Keep your eye on the linemen. Are they backing up to pass block or are they driving forward to create the hole needed for a running play?

Often these actions will give you quick keys to the play as it develops. The offense will be doing its best, however, to disguise its intentions as long as possible. During a play action pass the quarterback appears to hand the ball off before dropping back to pass and the linemen drive off the line to make the defense think it will be a run. The receivers would fake blocks before running their pass patterns. While they are fooling the defense they are also fooling you, and it should take some time before you learn to recognize a play action pass before it develops. But once you have figured out that the offense intends to pass, locate the receivers and follow their routes.

There are four types of pass action which are usually seen in a game:

The Drop Back Pass

The drop back pass is the easiest to pick out because no attempt is made to disguise the play. (*See Figure 4.*) It is used on obvious passing situations, such as second or third down when long yardage is needed to get to a first down. The quarterback takes the snap and drops straight back from the center. Offensive linemen assume a pass-blocking position, hitting their opponents and staying between them and the quarterback as long as possible. They will drop back to form a protective pocket of linemen around the quarterback. The running backs will either stay in the backfield and help block the rushing linemen or will go out as additional pass receivers. The quarterback stays in the protection of the pocket while he looks downfield and then passes the ball.

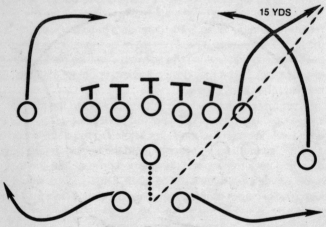

Figure 4. The drop back pass.

The Sprint-Out Pass (Rollout Pass)

As the name of the play indicates, the quarterback takes the snap from center and sprints out of the pocket, either to his left or his right. While on the run, the quarterback makes the decision whether to run or pass. If his intended receiver is open right away, he will usually throw for a short gain of 6 to 8 yards in the flat. (*See Figure 5.*) If the receiver is covered, the quarterback can choose to pull the ball down and run with it. This becomes one of the most interesting plays in the passing game because the quarterback must quickly decide whether he should become a passer or a runner. You can make this decision with the quarterback. Once the quarterback takes the snap from center and sprints out, look for the receiver in the flat, see whether the receiver is open or covered, and then decide whether the quarterback should take the option to run or to pass. The sprint-out pass may be used in any situation because the quarterback has the option to make it a run or a pass.

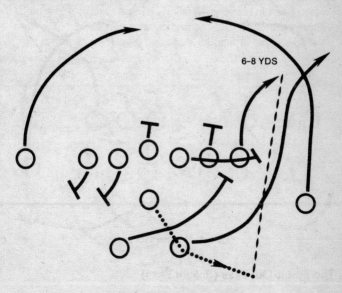

6–8 YDS

Figure 5. The sprint-out pass.

The Play Action Pass

The play action pass is the most difficult to recognize because it is actually designed to look like a running play right up until the pass is thrown. The quarterback fakes a handoff to a running back, who puts his head down and runs as if he is carrying the ball. Every member of the offensive team is trying to make the play look like a running play as long as possible. The offensive linemen will block aggressively, just as they would for a run, and the receiver will attempt to convince the defense that he is going to block or that he is loafing on the play. In the backfield, the quarterback tries to hide the ball with his body for as long as possible while looking downfield, picking out an open receiver and throwing the ball. The key to this play is the element of surprise, and it is most effective when used in running situations such as second down with short yardage to go for a first down, when the defense (and the spectator) anticipate a running play. (*See Figure 6.*)

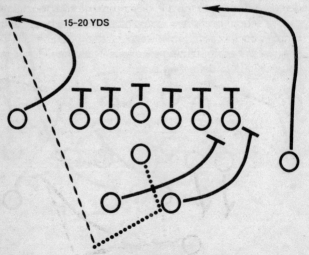

15–20 YDS

Figure 6. The play action pass.

The Halfback Running Pass

The halfback running pass is the most sophisticated of the play action passes. One of the reasons Paul Hornung was such a great player with the legendary Green Bay Packers was his ability to execute this play. It is designed to look exactly like a sweep. (*See Figure 7.*) The quarterback actually hands the ball off to the running back. The ball carrier then puts the ball under his arm and runs a few steps to convince the defense that it is going to be a running play. If he shows pass at all in his first three or four steps after he takes the handoff he will destroy the surprise element of the play. Meanwhile the receiver, who at first added to the deception by appearing to be loafing or blocking, tries to get behind the defensive backs downfield. Once the ball carrier has faked the sweep he pulls up and throws deep to the receiver.

The halfback running pass is looked upon as a big play or a "home run" or touchdown play. It is designed to lure the defensive players to the line of scrimmage so a touchdown can be scored over them and is often effective because the running back is not normally expected to pass the ball. The play works best in running situations when the defense must commit itself to defending the run.

Figure 7. The halfback running pass.

HOW TO RECOGNIZE PASS PATTERNS

One of the most picturesque plays in the game of football is the great reception by a gifted receiver. The movements of a top receiver making a difficult catch have been compared to those of a ballet dancer. Lynn Swann, who recently retired from the Pittsburgh Steelers, is an excellent example of someone who combined the grace and skill of a ballet dancer with the acrobatic movements of a top receiver. In order to best appreciate the abilities of the receiver, the student and fan should recognize the type of pattern the receiver is attempting to run and the way he is attempting to get open. The same play may be run different ways depending on the defense. Against man-to-man coverage, the receiver will attempt to make a series of moves to evade the man covering him. Against zone coverages he will look for the open spot or the *seam*.

The Fly Pattern or Streak Pattern (The Bomb)

The fly or streak pattern is most effective when used by a receiver to get open against a man-to-man defense. The receiver sprints straight at the defensive man, makes a quick fake as if he were going to break right or left, and then tries to sprint right past the defender. A receiver with good speed (4.5 seconds for 40 yards) can run this pattern to devastating effect. But no matter how fast he runs, he must convince the defensive back that he is going to break in or out before he can sprint past him and get open deep. (*See Figure 8.*)

The Out Pattern

The out pattern is also most effective against the man-to-man defense. The receiver runs directly at the defensive back (usually at his inside shoulder), which forces the defensive back to start back and turn to the inside to protect against the long bomb. Once the receiver has his man turned to the inside or moving back, he then breaks to the outside and looks for the ball. (*See Figure 8.*)

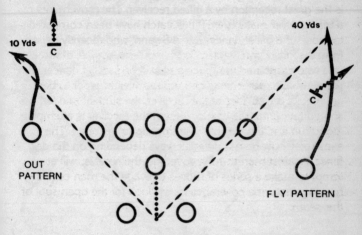

Figure 8. The fly or streak pattern and the out pass pattern against a man-to-man defense.

The Sideline Pattern

The sideline pattern is the pattern used most frequently by receivers when they want to make sure they get a certain gain on a play. The receiver sprints down the field to a predetermined point (often 8 to 10 yards). The receiver then executes a 90-degree or square cut, breaking sharply to the sideline, and the quarterback times his pass to reach him just before he steps out of bounds. The keys to completing the sideline pattern are the ability of the receiver to make a good cut and the ability of the passer to deliver the ball just before the receiver goes out of bounds. When this play is executed properly it is almost impossible to defend. (*See Figure 9.*)

Because the game clock stops after the receiver steps out of bounds with the ball, the sideline pattern is especially useful when the team is attempting to gain yardage and stop the clock at the same time. It is an integral part of the *two minute drill*, a series of plays designed to move the ball while conserving as much game time as possible. So watch for the sideline pass when a team has a long distance to go at the end of the first or second half and there is little time left.

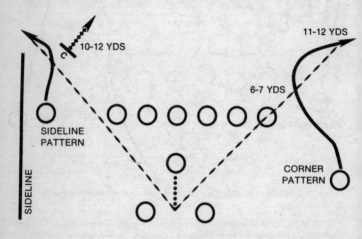

Figure 9. The sideline pattern and the corner pattern against a man-to-man defense.

The Post Pattern

On a post play the receiver starts straight down the field for 10 to 12 yards and then breaks at an angle toward the goal posts. In most cases, the receiver will make a slight fake to the outside before he breaks in toward the goalposts. Against man-to-man coverage this will often get him open, and if the passer can get the ball to the receiver just after he breaks, it can be very difficult to defend. When the receiver is running this pattern against a zone defense, the quarterback will try to lay the ball in the seam, just beyond the linebackers and in front of the deeper defensive backs. (*See Figure 10.*)

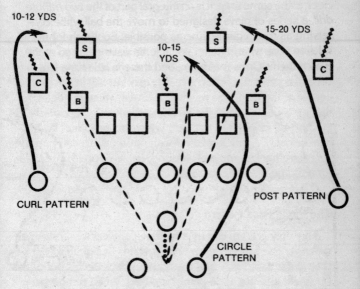

Figure 10. The post pattern and the curl pattern against a zone defense. The ball is thrown in the seam between the deep backs and the linebackers. The circle pattern by the running back against the linebackers.

The Curl Pattern

The curl pattern can be very effective against both the man-to-man defense or the zone defense. The receiver sprints straight at the defensive man, drives him back and then curls back (either in or out) toward the quarterback. The ball should be thrown before the receiver starts his curl, so that the receiver can catch the ball just as he makes his turn. As with any successful pass, split-second timing between the passer and the receiver is essential. To complete this pass against a zone defense, it must be thrown over the linebackers and in front of the defensive backs.

The Corner Pass Pattern

Look for the wide receiver to sprint straight down the field for 6 or 7 yards and then fake as if he were going to run a post pattern. Once the defensive back moves to the inside to defend against the post move, the receiver will break for the corner of the field. The receiver must convince the defender that he is going to run the post and then make a good cut to the outside in order to get free. Watch his head and body fakes closely. A quick receiver with good moves can turn the defensive back completely around, get wide open, and break for a big gain. (*See Figure 9.*)

The Circle Pass Pattern

This play is often run by a halfback against a man-to-man defense. The wide receivers run patterns designed to draw their defenders away, and the running back circles out of the backfield into the open part of the field. When run properly, it isolates the linebacker so that he must cover the faster running back, resulting in a mismatch. Against a zone, this pattern will be run toward the open spots in the defense. Look for this play when a team has a fast back who can catch the ball well. (*See Figure 10.*)

The Comeback Pass Pattern

The comeback pass pattern is another play which is virtually impossible to stop when the route is run correctly. Again, the receiver must convince the defensive back that he is going to run a deep pattern by sprinting directly at him. Once he has started the defender deep, he plants his outside foot and drives back toward the passer. He should make this move after driving the defender 14 or 15 yards downfield. Against zone defenses, the receiver will be looking to find the seam before making his cut back. The key to completing this and any pass play is for both the quarterback and the receiver to know exactly where on the field the cut will be made, so that the football can actually be thrown *before* the receiver changes direction. (*See Figure 11.*)

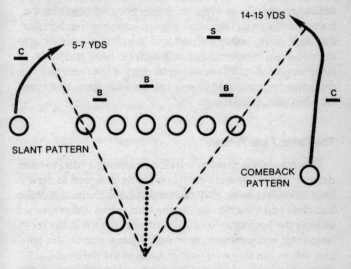

Figure 11. The slant pattern and the comeback pattern against a man-to-man defense.

The Slant Pass Pattern

This play is exactly what its name implies. The wide receiver takes off, runs two or three steps at the defender and slants down the field at approximately a 45-degree angle. A good quarterback will get the ball to the receiver as soon as he makes his cut. This play is run at full speed because the receiver will only be open for a matter of seconds; to work it must take advantage of the movement of the defensive back as he adjusts to defend against the deep pass.

Our discussion to this point has been concerned with the individual patterns by a single player. But on any given play, as many as five receivers might be downfield looking for the ball. And as many as eight defenders trying to keep them from catching it. So the offensive team designs each pass play to spread out those defenders as much as possible and to draw them away from the primary or choice receiver as he runs his pattern. With an understanding of the diversity of patterns, you can begin to see how they can be used to complement one another.

The Swing Pass Pattern (with Complementary Patterns)

The swing pass is a short drop-off pass to one of the running backs just behind the line of scrimmage. The key to this pass is not the yardage that is gained in the air but the yardage that is gained after the football is caught. As in the circle pattern, the swing pass gives the back a chance to elude the defending linebacker and break open for a long gain. This play can be used to effect against both the man-to-man or the zone defense whenever the defense concentrates its coverage on the wide receivers and the tight end, because the running back gets a chance to run with the ball in the open field. And any time a good running back gets to use his speed and elusiveness in the open with tacklers scattered over the field, there is chance for a long gain. (*See Figure 12.*)

When this pass is thrown, the quarterback must make sure that he throws the pass forward, and that the receiver is farther down the field than the quarterback. If the ball is thrown laterally or backwards, the throw is considered a *lateral* and will become a free ball if dropped by the receiver. When a forward pass is dropped, it is dead; and the ball is returned to the original line of scrimmage for the next play. But when a lateral is dropped, it is considered a free ball and can be recovered by either team.

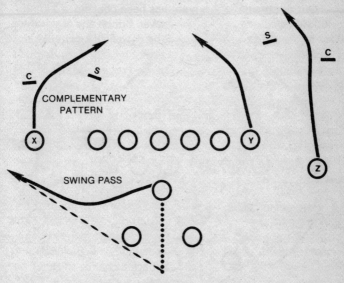

Figure 12. The Swing or flare pattern against a man-to-man defense. The complementary pattern clears the area of the defensive backs. (Receiver X.)

The Checkoff Pass

The checkoff pass pattern is similar to the swing pattern or flare pattern. It is called a checkoff because it usually represents the second or third option of a play; the quarterback tosses the ball to one of the running backs if he cannot find an open receiver downfield. (*See Figure 13.*) It should be thrown softly and laid out in front of the receiver so that he can run under the ball. The checkoff pattern is most often run by one of the backs, who will break into this pattern after he has blocked for the passer. In such a case, the back is acting like a safety valve or outlet for the quarterback; if the pressure from the defensive linemen and linebackers gets too heavy and the protection of the pocket starts to break down, the quarterback knows he can just flip the ball out to the runner.

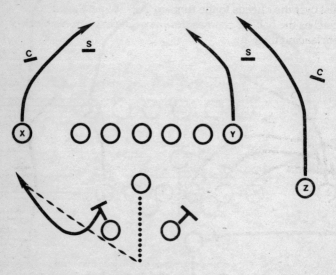

Figure 13. The checkoff pattern. The complementary patterns take the defensive backs deep.

The Screen Pass

The screen pass is most effective against a defense which is concentrating on rushing the passer. (*See Figure 14.*) The quarterback takes his normal drop back from the center and the wide receivers run deep patterns in order to attempt to spread out the defense. The running back first blocks but then leaves the charging linemen and runs a pattern similar

— 34 —

to the checkoff. The offensive linemen on the side where the pass is to be thrown start to block but then let the defense past them and run out in front of the receiver to form a blocking screen. As with the swing pass, the wide receivers run deep patterns which draw the defensive backs from the play. The quarterback acts as if he is looking to throw a long pass, retreats to evade the onrushing linemen, and throws the ball just over their heads to the running back. When the back catches the ball, he charges down the sideline with his blockers leading the way.

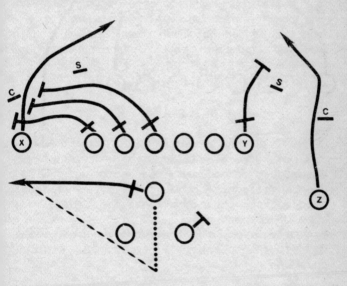

Figure 14. The screen pass. X clears the area of the deep backs, Y becomes a blocker, and Z holds the deep backs on his side of the field.

When it is properly set up and used against a defense which is being too aggressive, the screen pass can be a big yardage play. Look for the screen pass on second and third downs when long yardage is needed for a first down or against a defense which is attempting an all-out pass rush. The key to the screen pass is to convince the defense that the pass rushers have indeed trapped the quarterback for a loss. Once the quarterback has drawn the pass rushers deep into the backfield and lobbed the ball over their heads, the running back will have an open field in which to maneuver.

It is interesting to note that the complementary patterns of the wide receivers are the same for both the screen pass and the swing pass but they are run for different purposes. In each case, the receivers run deep patterns to take their defenders away from the short zones. In the swing pattern, however, the complementary patterns are run to force the defense to cover the halfback with a linebacker. On the screen pass, their purpose is to create running room once the pass is caught.

TRICK PLAY PASSES

Some of the most spectacular plays in football are trick play passes. There are trick plays to be run from any formation and their success usually depends upon deception and the element of surprise. In general they involve more complicated ball handling than most plays, so there is more chance of the offensive team losing the ball on a turnover. But because they also offer a better chance for a long gain, you should look for these plays whenever a team is in need of a quick score.

The Flea Flicker

The flea flicker is a catch-all phrase for a number of such plays. The most common is a pass combined with a lateral. The quarterback drops back to pass and throws to a receiver who has run a curl pattern. When the pass is completed and the defensive backs converge to make the tackle, the receiver pitches a short lateral to a running back who has been trailing the play. If the back is in good position and can catch the ball without losing his momentum, he should have open field ahead because the defensive backs have concentrated on the original receiver. This particular play was used by Oklahoma University against Nebraska on national television in a game which decided the championship of the Big Eight Conference. Although Oklahoma was behind with little time remaining, they were able to execute this play for a touchdown and win both the game and the championship. (*See Figure 15.*)

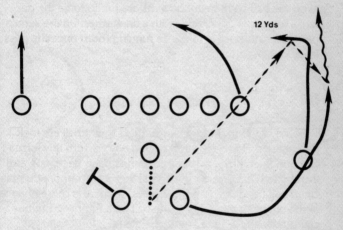

Figure 15. The flea flicker. A curl pattern by the wide receiver with a lateral to the trailing back.

The Throw Back (Flea Flicker)

The key to the throw back is that it appears to be a running play. The quarterback hands the ball off to the halfback on what seems to be a sweep right and does a poor fake after the handoff so the defense can see he no longer has the ball. The running back tucks the ball under his arm and runs hard toward the sideline, drawing the defense up to play the run. He then stops, whirls, and passes the ball back across the field. There the quarterback catches the ball and throws it deep downfield to a receiver who has slipped behind the defense. (*See Figure 16.*)

On this play, it is important that the throw back to the quarterback be a lateral. If it is thrown forward, it will count as a forward pass, and it is not legal to throw two forward passes on the same play. In another variation of the throwback, the runner takes the handoff and fakes a run into the line before flipping the ball back to the quarterback.

Figure 16. The throw back, a fake running play (sweep) by the running back with a crossfield lateral back to the quarterback and a long pass to the wide receiver who runs a deep pattern after faking a block.

The End Around Pass

The end around pass is another trick play pass based on deception. It too begins as a run, but it becomes a pass at the last possible moment. The running back starts on what appears to be a sweep but then hands the football off to a wide receiver who is coming the other direction in a reverse pattern. The receiver takes the handoff and circles back through the backfield in the opposite direction, running full tilt as if it were an end around play. But after a few steps, he stops short and looks downfield for an open receiver.

Meanwhile, the other wide receiver makes a move toward the center of the field to cause the defense to think he is a lead blocker for the end around run. It is important that he masquerade as a blocker as long as he possibly can. He should run directly at the middle linebacker long enough to convince the corner back and the safety to come up and defend against the run, and then break out 25 or 30 yards deep behind them and look for the pass. (*See Figure 17.*)

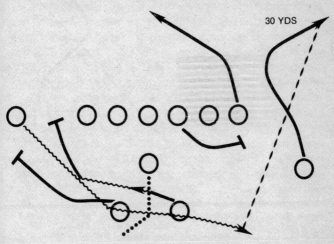

Figure 17. The end around pass.

The end around pass can be set up by a successful end around run (a play of similar design where, instead of throwing the ball, the receiver keeps it and runs up the sideline). If a wide receiver has made good yardage on a previous play, the defense will be forced to react quickly to the running threat when he gets his hands on the ball. But this is a difficult play to execute and requires a receiver with a rare combination of skills. He must not only have the speed to be a breakaway running threat, but must also have an arm strong and accurate enough to reach the receiver 30 yards upfield.

When you are at a game, pay attention to the play of individual receivers. Notice how one executes his moves. When he runs a sideline pattern are his cuts square and true? Is he able to make his moves at top speed or does he lose his momentum? Is he making the same fake every time so that the defender can anticipate his actions or does the receiver vary his motions to keep the defense guessing? Has he been running short patterns to set the defender up for a long pass? If you are watching the game on television, study the isolated shots of wide receivers which are being used more and more often, where one camera is assigned to keep track of the receiver from the time the ball is snapped and a replay is shown after the play is over, giving you an opportunity to follow his pattern from beginning to end. This procedure, which has become a standard procedure on Monday Night Football and NCAA College Football telecasts, also gives television viewers their best chances to keep track of the defensive coverages.

When a receiver is consistently getting open for a certain kind of pass, look for the defensive team to make adjustments and then look for the offense to take advantage of those adjustments. If the end is getting open for long passes, the back will have to start further down the field or get some assistance from other defenders. If he backs up, it will leave him vulnerable to shorter patterns. If he gets help from other

defensive backs, the offense can exploit that by passing to
other areas of the field which now have less coverage.

PASSING AGAINST A
ZONE DEFENSE

Throughout the game, the offense will analyze the alignment of the defense, study the adjustments it has made, and
try to call the plays which will give them the best chance of
advancing the ball. Each offensive play contains specific assignments for each player; every man is involved on every
play in the effort to exploit the weaknesses of the defense.
This is particularly important when trying to beat a zone defense, when the defensive linebackers and backs are not
assigned to cover individual players from the time the ball is
snapped but instead are given the responsibility of defending
areas of the field, or zones. When someone runs into a defensive back's zone, he will then adjust to defend against that
player's pattern. If that receiver leaves the zone, the back does
not follow him. Instead, the responsibility for defending him
shifts to the defender whose zone he entered.

A zone defense makes it possible for two slower defensive
backs to cover a speedy receiver who would outdistance
them in a man-to-man footrace. When passing against such
a defense, success relies not so much on the individual effort
of the receiver but on coordinated positions and pass patterns of the offense. There are two basic techniques for passing against a zone defense.

The Flood Pattern (Flooding a Zone)

In a zone, the defense has chosen to spread its defenders
across the field. By flooding a zone, the offense overloads a
particular area, sending many receivers to that area so that it

is impossible for the defense to cover them all. With receivers carefully spaced throughout a zone, the defensive player cannot cover each person closely and at least one receiver should be open for a well-thrown pass.

The flood pattern can be combined effectively with a sprint-out pass. (*See Figure 18.*) On this play, the quarterback sprints out with the ball held in the ready position so he can throw instantly when he sees an open receiver. The wide receiver (z) goes to deepest part of the zone, the tight end (y) goes to the short zone, and the running back runs a flare pattern in the shallow flat zone. As with any sprint-out pass, the quarterback has the option of running if he decides that his receivers are too close together and have not flooded the zone properly by the time he is ready to throw.

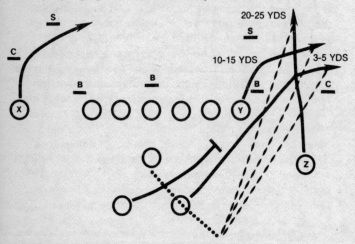

Figure 18. Flooding a zone. The receiver (Z) goes to the deep zone, Y goes to the short zone, and the running back runs a flare pattern in the flat zone.

Clearing the Zone

The trick to clearing a zone is to lure the zone's defender out of his position. One receiver runs a pattern through a zone to draw the defensive man to one side so that a second receiver can go to that same area and be open. One frequently used method is to send wide receivers long to take the defensive backs deep and then have the tight end cut across "under" the coverage in the short area of the zone. The tight end must maneuver quickly to find the open space behind the linebackers. If he runs too deep, the defensive backs will have a chance to recover and knock away the pass; if he runs a pattern which is too close to the linebackers, they can drop back and make the play. (*See Figure 19.*)

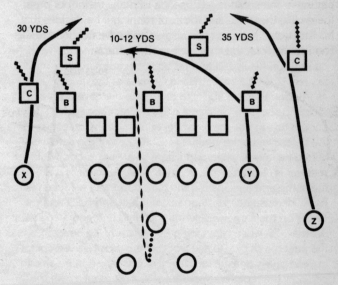

Figure 19. Clearing the zone. X takes the defensive backs deep, Z holds the defensive backs deep on his side, and the tight end (Y) come across and finds the open area.

Finding the Seams

In a zone defense, each member of a defensive backfield assumes responsibility for an area of the field. When the ball is snapped, each will drop back to the center of his assigned zone as he prepares to cover the receiver who runs into his area. When the defenders spread out in their zones, spaces open up between them in the "seams" which separate the various zones. The receivers should run their patterns to those spaces where there is the most distance between defenders. The more space, the more time it will take the defenders to run to cover up the receiver, and the better the chance of completing the pass. It is in these seams that the zone is most vulnerable to attack. As mentioned earlier, it is in these areas that receivers look to make their cuts in patterns like the circle and the cutback.

The way a receiver runs his pattern is dictated by the way he is being played by the defense. Against a man-to-man, he can rely on his speed and his ability to outmaneuver the defender. Against a zone, the elusiveness of the receiver is not as important as his ability to recognize the coverages and to locate the seams. On many plays the receiver is given different options to choose from depending on the reactions of the defensive backs, and he must figure out the defense before he knows when and where to make his cut. While the receiver is "reading" the defense, the quarterback is doing the same and anticipating the play along with his receiver. Every defense has weak points and a quarterback and receiver on the same wavelength can find an open area in any defense. So when watching a game, study the coverages and the patterns of play to see whether the receivers are operating effectively against the defense. You will soon be able to see how the receivers vary routes in accordance with the defenses they are facing.

Basic Rules in Regard to Pass Patterns

It is important that you understand the out-of-bounds rule. In professional football, the receiver must have *both* feet inside the playing area after he has gained possession of the ball. College football players are only required to have one foot inside the line after they have possession of the ball. If the receiver's foot touches the out-of-bounds line before the catch is made, he is ruled out of bounds, and the catch does not count. No receiver is allowed to run out of bounds and then return to the playing field and catch the ball.

One of the most controversial and least understood rules in football is the rule governing offensive and defensive pass interference. Simply stated, the receiver must go after the ball and cannot hold, push, or block the defender to keep him from getting the ball while the ball is in the air. By the same token, once the ball is in the air the defensive man is only allowed to go after the football. He cannot push, hold, or block the receiver to keep him from making the catch or he will be charged with defensive pass interference. (After the receiver has touched the ball, the defense is allowed to hit him to jar the ball loose.)

Part of the reason it is controversial is that it requires a subjective decision by the referee. If the defender and receiver bump into each other while going for the ball, then he determines whether it was "incidental conduct", which can go unpunished, or if it is interference, who is at fault. The pass interference rule puts a lot of pressure on the defense. Defensive pass interference can be one of the most costly penalties in the game because the offense is allowed an automatic first down at the point of the foul. If the interference occurs on a fly or streak pattern 40 yards downfield, the offense can gain 40 yards and a first down without even completing the pass.

The defender may make contact with the receiver before the ball is thrown. But he may only hit him once beyond a point five yards downfield and cannot block the receiver down at the line of scrimmage. (Blocking the receiver at the line of scrimmage is legal in high school or intercollegiate football.)

Any contact between the receiver and the defensive man is illegal after the ball is in the air.

It is also a penalty if the offense blocks a defender downfield on a pass play before the ball is caught. This rule, which applies to both linemen and receivers, means that one offensive player cannot act as a shield for a fellow receiver who is going for the ball by blocking or impeding the defense in anyway.

Multiple Offensive Formations

Up to this point, we have diagrammed pass patterns from one formation only, split backs. But there are almost as many formations as there are pass patterns, and the spectator should learn to recognize them. When the offense lines up for the snap, try to identify the formation and to locate the eligible receivers and the key running backs. Often the positioning of the ballplayers will give you a clue to the team's intentions. Figures 20 through 35 give some examples of pass patterns run from various formations.

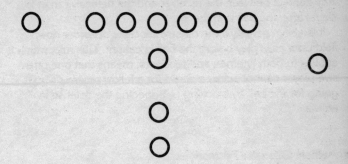

Figure 20. The I formation, with both running backs lined up directly behind the quarterback.

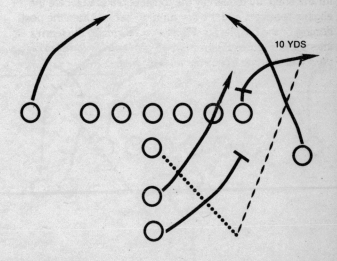

Figure 21. The play action pass from the I. The quarterback fakes to the upback, drops back, and passes to the tight end in the flat.

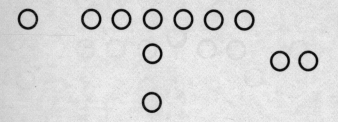

Figure 22. The double flanker. This formation uses only one back, adding an extra wide receiver. Because only seven offensive players may be on the line at one time, both right flankers line up off the line of scrimmage.

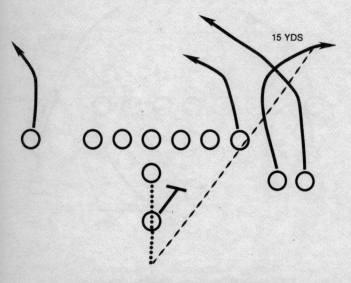

Figure 23. The crossing pattern from the double flanker.

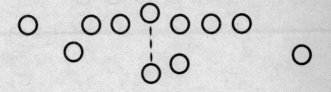

Figure 24. The shotgun. This formation is used primarily in passing situations. The quarterback lines up in the backfield, and the ball is hiked to him in the air.

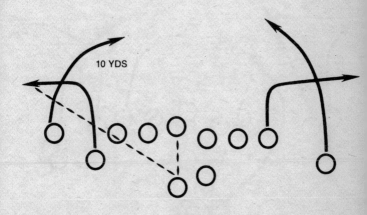

Figure 25. The sideline pattern from the shotgun.

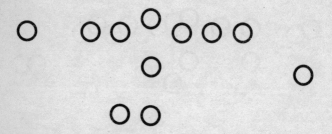

Figure 26. The pro set formation, with one back directly behind the quarterback and the second off to the side.

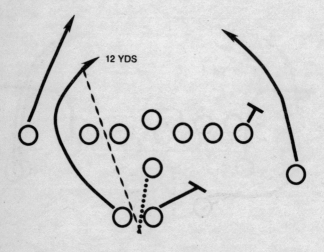

Figure 27. The circle pattern from the pro set.

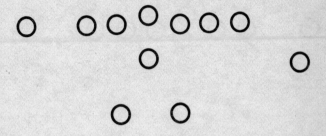

Figure 28. The pro set formation with split backs.

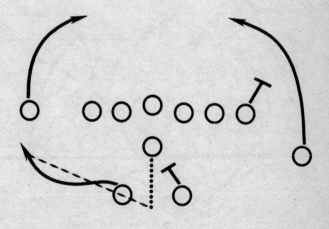

Figure 29. The swing pattern from split backs.

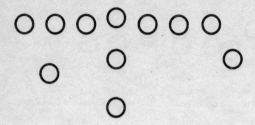

Figure 30. The wing T formation.

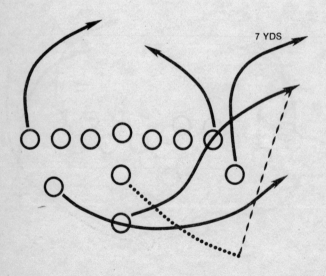

Figure 31. The sprint-out pass from the wing T formation (run or pass option).

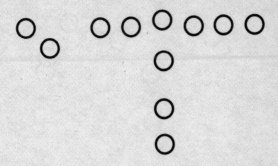

Figure 32. The slot formation, with the flanker set off the line of scrimmage just inside the split end.

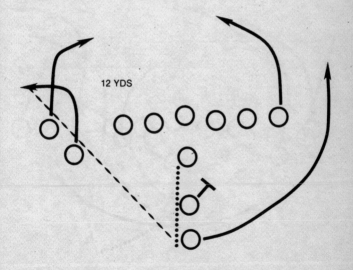

Figure 33. The basic out pattern from the slot formation.

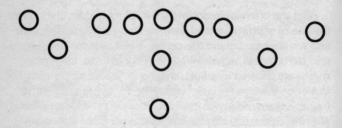

Figure 34. The double slot formation.

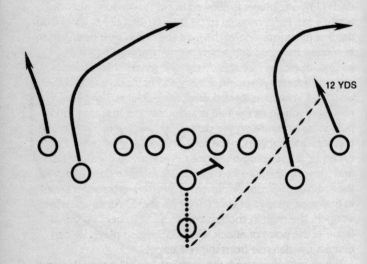

Figure 35. The curl pass from the double slot formation.

The Use of Motion to Change the Set

After the offensive team breaks from its huddle, they go to the line of scrimmage and assume their positions. The quarterback lines up behind the center, looks over the defense, and starts to call signals. While he is doing this, his teammates are allowed to adjust, shifting into their set position. But once the quarterback yells "Set," his teammates must freeze. A team must hold its *set position* for at least one second, after which the ball can be hiked. This gives the defensive players, who are not required to come to a complete stop, an opportunity to react to the final set positions before the play begins.

The offense is allowed one exception to the set rule. On each play, one player is allowed to go "in motion" after the team is set. He is allowed to be moving laterally or away from the line of scrimmage at the time the ball is snapped. A man in motion may be used when the offense wants to shift an additional receiver to one side or the other. This is usually accomplished by sending a running back who starts in the backfield in motion toward one of the sidelines and having him turn upfield as the ball is snapped. The man in motion puts extra pressure on the defense by forcing them to make adjustments right up to the time the ball is put in play. For example, if a running back goes in motion to the right side and turns up the field in the area between the tight end and the wide receiver, the defense must then cover three receivers in that area instead of two. (*See Figure 36.*) As an offensive weapon, the man in motion can be used to beef up the offense at the point of attack. On misdirection plays, he can distract the defense from the real target.

When motion is used, the quarterback will normally signal for the man to start by raising his heel. If the man passes behind the signal caller he will pat him on the backside to communicate his position. Plays which include a man in motion usually take a bit longer to get off, so the quarterback must make sure that the team sets up quickly in order to get the play off within the allotted time.

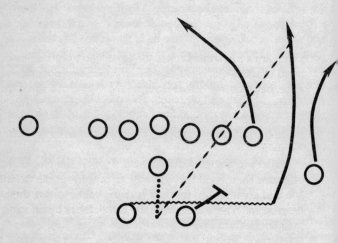

Figure 36. The use of a man in motion toward the tight end to change the offensive set. (Three receivers on the same side at the snap of the ball).

THE RUNNING GAME

A team's rushing attack is the foundation of its offense. A good running game is essential to establishing offensive balance, because the offense can be most effective when the defense must prepare to defend against both the pass and the run. If the defense knows that their opponent cannot move the ball on the ground, then they will overplay against the pass.

The key to a successful running attack is the play of the offensive linemen. If they are able to overpower the defensive line and create room for their running backs to run, then the defense will have to reinforce the run defense by bringing their linebackers and defensive backs closer to the line of scrimmage. This in turn will leave them more vulnerable to pass plays. However, if the defensive line is able to hold their own, their teammates can play deeper and concentrate on keeping the wide receivers covered. An offense that cannot make consistent yardage on running plays will be forced to throw the ball against a defense that will be stacked to stop the pass.

At the beginning of the game, watch the two lines play and see if the "war in the trenches" is being won by the defense or the offense. See where the defense is at the end of running plays. Are they in the backfield, or have they been pushed five yards downfield? Are the running backs making 7 yards every time they carry the ball, or are they being held to two? Can the ball carrier gain yardage on sweeps, or are they only effective running up the middle? If one line dominates, you can expect the loser to make adjustments and pay the price. .

As you become more familiar with running plays, it will help you to evaluate the ability of a running back. Is he taking advantage of the "daylight" available when he runs a sweep? Can he cut into a hole without losing speed? Does he stay behind his blockers and use them to shield himself from would-be tacklers, or does he run past them into the arms of the defensive men? If he is gaining yards, is it because the defense is concentrating on stopping the pass or because of the work of the offensive line? When he is caught, is it because he was slow in the backfield or because the tackler simply outplayed a blocker? As you learn to recognize the points where the offense is being effective or is breaking down, you can start to notice and then anticipate the adjustments that are made during the game.

Here are some of the basic running plays you can expect to see:

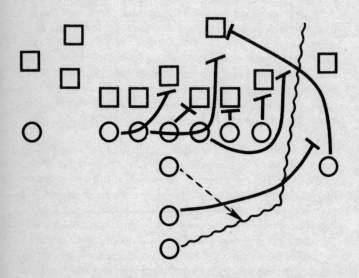

Figure 37. The pitch sweep play against the 4-3 defense.

The Pitch Sweep Play

One of the most colorful plays in football is the pitch sweep from the I formation. On this play, the student of the game should watch the blocking of the offensive linemen and the other backs as well as moves of the ball carrier. The lead block by the fullback is particularly important, and the blocks by the pulling guards are key to the success of the play. This play is a variation of the "student body right" or "student body left" made famous at U.S.C. in the last decade. (*See Figure 37.*) The deep back in the I formation turns up the field behind the blocks of the fullback and the right guard and then "runs to daylight," which means he does not run to a pre-determined hole but to whatever opening appears.

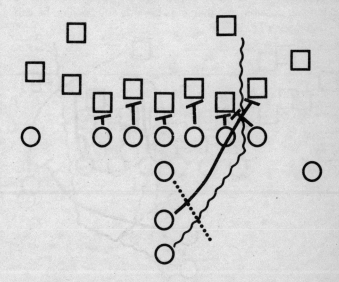

Figure 38. The off tackle play against the 3-4 defense.

I Formation Off Tackle Play

The I formation back (the deep back) breaks off of the block of the fullback or blocking back and turns up the field inside of the defensive end. The quarterback first fakes the ball to the fullback before handing off to the I back, who runs to daylight. (*See Figure 38.*)

The I Formation Blast Play

The shortest distance between two points is also the least complicated, and the I formation blast play is created for short yardage situations. Pitting strength against strength, the I back follows the blocking of the fullback right up the middle. The linemen fire straight at the defensive men and block them any way they can; the back runs behind the fullback as long as possible and then cuts towards any opening he can find. (*See Figure 39.*)

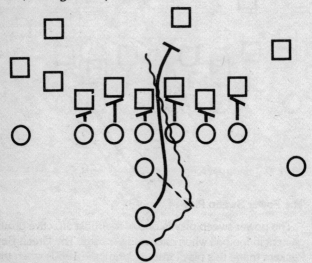

Figure 39. The blast play against the 3-4 defense.

The Trap Play

The trap play is effective when used against a hard-charging line. The play is so called because it uses the defensive player's quickness to cause him to fall into a trap. This is a sucker play, in which the player is presented with an opening and is allowed to penetrate through the line and into the backfield but is then screened off from the side and the ball carrier runs to the space that is left in the area the player had vacated. (*See Figure 40.*) A well-executed trap can negate a defensive line's quickness and can actually force it to slow down its reaction time.

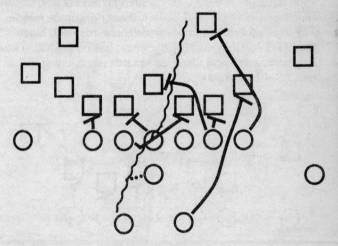

Figure 40. The trap play against the 4-3 defense (pro set, split backs formation).

The Power Sweep Play

The power sweep play is one of the most effective ground gainers in football when executed properly. The Green Bay Packers made this play famous during the 1960s when they dominated the National Football League. The ball carrier starts to run wide around end but then turns up the field as quickly as possible so that he is gaining ground and not running laterally. Both guards "pull" (meaning that instead of blocking straight ahead they actually pull back from the line of scrimmage and sprint out in front of the runner) and lead the play so that there is a strong blocking wall for the ball carrier. This play differs from the quick toss sweep in that the quarterback does not throw the ball into the air but takes it out and hands it off instead. (*See Figure 41.*)

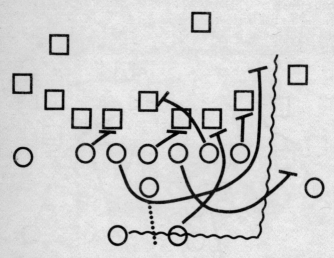

Figure 41. The power sweep against the 4-3 defense (pro set, split backs formation).

The Quick Toss Sweep

The quick toss sweep is designed to get the ball to the running back quickly so that he can run with outside position on the defense and turn up the field in a hurry. The sweep is often run after faking a trap play, which has the effect of drawing the defense toward the center of the field. The fullback will run a trap and the quarterback will fake a handoff to him as he sticks his head down and runs up the middle. As the defense responds, the quarterback whirls and pitches the ball out to the halfback, who by now has begun his move to the outside. Unlike the power sweep, the tackle pulls out as the lead blocker since he sets up closer to the outside and in better position and because the guards are faking trap blocks. The quick toss can be a big gainer, but because of the pitch there is also more chance of mishandling the ball than there is on a handoff. As with any play which delays getting the ball over the line of scrimmage, there is more chance of getting trapped and tackled for a loss of yards if the defense diagnoses the play and reacts quickly. (*See Figure 42.*)

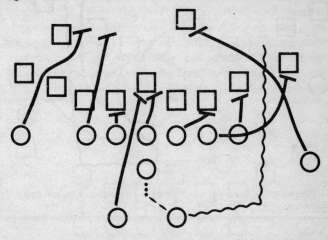

Figure 42. The quick toss sweep against the 4-3 defense (pro set, split backs formation).

Runs that Complement the Pass

There are some running plays designed specifically to complement the passing game. They are called to take advantage of a defense which is putting an all-out rush to get pressure on the passer and are used to keep the defenses aware of the running play. When these plays work, it is more difficult for the defensive linemen and linebackers to charge the quarterback with reckless abandon.

The Draw Play

Just as the play action pass is a pass designed to look like a run, the draw play is a run designed to look like a pass. In this play, the quarterback drops straight back as if to pass while the running backs simulate pass blocks. The offensive linemen also show pass by executing pass blocks. As they back up and appear to be setting up a pocket, they will be trying to create running room up the middle by allowing the linemen to get to the outside. The wide receivers run deep pass patterns which will drive the defensive backs deep and away from the play. As the quarterback backs into the pocket on what appears to be a drop back pass, however, he hands the ball off to one the running backs. The back takes the handoff and "runs to daylight." (*See Figure 43.*)

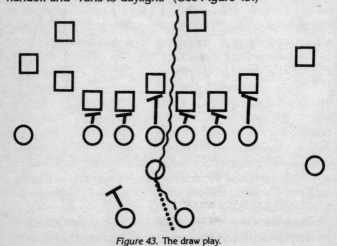

Figure 43. The draw play.

The draw is used in the opposite circumstances from the play action: the play action is most effective when the defense is overplaying the run, the draw when it is expecting a pass. Each play also can be used to set up the other. When the draw has been successful, the faked handoff of the play action pass can "freeze" the linebackers, forcing them to delay their rush while they look to make sure the back does not have the ball. When the play action has worked, the defense must pay attention to the quarterback even after he has held out the ball as if to hand off.

The Quarterback Draw

This play is particularly effective with a quarterback who can pick a hole in the defense and find running room. The play begins with the quarterback dropping straight back as if to pass. He may even raise his arm and look downfield as if he is going to throw. The offensive linemen execute pass blocks; the wide receivers sprint down the field. But after looking downfield from his position in the pocket, the quarterback tucks the ball under his arm and runs upfield, again "running for daylight." As with the straight draw play, this play is most effective when the linemen can manipulate the defensive linemen and linebackers to take outside routes so that the space opens up in the middle. (*See Figure 44.*)

This planned running play should not be confused with the impromptu "scrambling" by the quarterback which happens when the quarterback is forced to run because he cannot find an open receiver to throw to or when the defensive pressure has broken down the protection of the pocket. Often a good running quarterback can make an excellent gain when scrambling because the defense has been spread out by the routes of the wide receivers and the pass blocking of the offensive linemen. Whenever you see a quarterback scrambling, it means that the defense has been doing its job, pressuring the quarterback and covering his receivers.

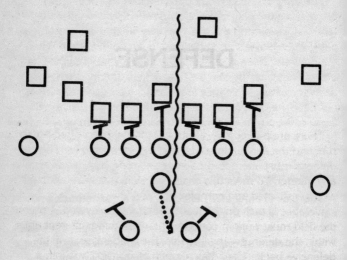

Figure 44: The quarterback draw.

These are the basic plays of any offense. Each team adds its own variations and special frills, but the football fan will recognize these as the "bread and butter" plays of any attack. Knowing them will help you understand a team's offensive strategy and ability.

DEFENSE

There are an endless number of plays that an offense can run, and the defense must be prepared for them all. The defense must attempt to counter and repel any attack from any quarter. To meet this challenge, defenses have become as sophisticated and complex as the offenses they face.

Defense is built on the team concept. All eleven players on the field must work in concert. There are three different units within the defense—the linemen, the linebackers, and the defensive backs. Each has his own responsibility within a given defense and his own assignment. A team defense is the result of a combination of assignments, which vary from play to play.

Defensive Formations

The 4–3 Defense is so named because of the presence of four down linemen in a three point stance (with one hand on the ground) and three linebackers behind them. Four defensive backs take positions behind them. This defense is sometimes called the *pro defense* because it is a basic defense in professional football. (*See Figure 45.*)

The 3–4 Defense is one of the more popular in the game today. Only three down linemen start on the line of scrimmage (with their hands on the ground); four linebackers and four defensive backs stand behind them. For many teams the 3–4 Defense has replaced the older, more orthodox 4–3 because of the advent of the new linebacker type in football.

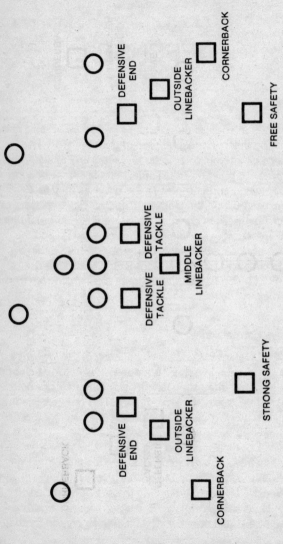

Figure 45. Defensive alignment for the 4-3 defense.

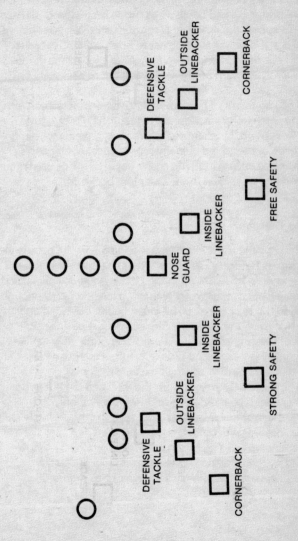

Figure 46. Defensive alignment for the 3-4 defense.

The new linebacker has the height but not the weight of the older prototype and he also has much more speed. Because of this speed, the new type is more effective on pass defense and is still able to rush the passer when a blitz is called (see page 72). In addition, the alignment of linebackers in the 3–4 enables them to pursue the ball more effectively on running plays. (*See Figure 46.*)

The alignment of the four defensive backs (the two corner-backs, the strong safety, and the free safety) is the same for a 3–4 or a 4–3. In recent years, however, teams have begun a practice of taking out a lineman or linebacker on passing downs and adding a fifth defensive back to provide even more speed and quickness in the defensive backfield.

Pass Defense

Perhaps the most effective weapon against the pass is the pass rush. Before he can throw a pass, the quarterback needs time to drop back, set up in the pocket, look downfield, and locate an open receiver. To get open, a receiver needs enough time to run his pattern, put a move on the defender, and break clear. If the defensive players can get past the protection of the offensive linemen quickly enough, they can literally rush the passer and reduce the time the quarterback and his receivers have in which to execute their play.

The basic pass rushes from the 4–3 and 3–4 defenses are executed by the defensive down linemen only. In the 4–3, the four down linemen charge at the quarterback while the other seven defensive players drop off into pass defense. (*See Figure 47.*) The basic pass rush from the 3–4 is executed by the three down linemen with four linebackers and four defensive backs in pass defense. (*See Figure 48.*)

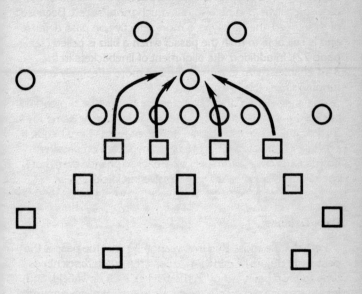

Figure 47. The basic four -man pass rush from the 4-3 defense (linebackers and defensive backs in zone pass defense).

Although the linemen are trying to "sack" the quarterback (tackle him before he releases the ball), they are also doing their job if they can force the quarterback to hurry his throw or throw high over them by penetrating the pocket or "cup". Notice how much time the quarterback has to throw the ball. Is he under pressure; is he being tackled right after every throw? Does he frequently have to scramble to avoid tacklers? When the defense is getting a good strong pass rush the offense must adjust. They can run shorter pass patterns so they take less time to develop. They can keep their running backs in the backfield as extra blockers instead of having them run patterns themselves. They can run draw plays to force the defense to slow down its rush. All of these, however, make it easier for the defensive backs to cover receivers and allow them to play closer to line of scrimmage, which puts them in better position to stop the run as well.

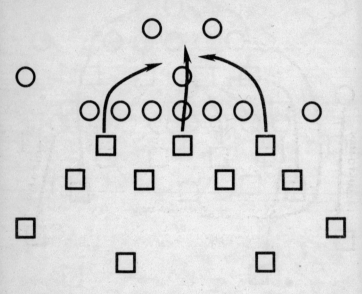

Figure 48. The basic three-man pass rush from the 3-4 defense (linebackers and defensive backs in zone pass defense).

It is an axiom of football that given time to throw, any quarterback can complete passes against any defense. If the defense is not able to get pressure on the quarterback, the pass rush can be increased by the use of "dogging" or "blitzing" linebackers or defensive backs. (*See Figure 49.*) Either the 4–3 or 3–4 pass rush can be increased by having additional players rush the quarterback—a team can "blitz" or "red dog" one, two, or three linebackers and a defensive back. (*See Figure 50.*) When this is done (and depending on how many players are left for pass defense and how effective the pass rush becomes), the zone pass defense is replaced with a man-to-man defense.

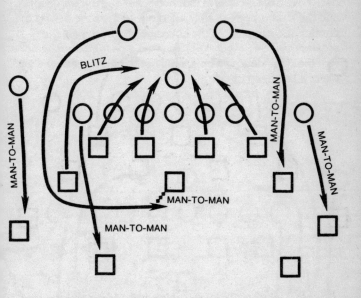

Figure 49. The "dogging" or "blitzing" linebacker from the 4-3 defense increases the rush from four men to five men with backs in man-to-man defense.

In certain situations, the defense may employ a safety blitz. (*See Figure 51.*) In a safety blitz, the free safety rushes the quarterback, and the other defensive backs are assigned man-to-man coverage.

"Jamming" or "chucking" a receiver is a pass defense technique used by defensive backs. The defender blocks the receiver at or near the line of scrimmage in order to hold him up or slow him down as he tries to run his pass pattern. Chucking can throw off the timing between the quarterback and receiver which is so important. The risk is that, if the receiver eludes the chuck, he can break free. Therefore it is often combined with "double coverage," where the corner- back covers the receiver in the short zone (8–12 yards deep), and the strong or free safety will move to the zone behind the cornerback and pick up the coverage should the receiver break deep. (*See Figure 52.*) To avoid a pass interference call, the defender must be careful not to hit the receiver after the ball has been thrown.

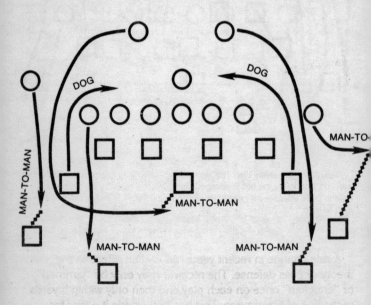

Figure 50. Both outside linebackers "dog" or "blitz" from the 4-3 to increase the rush from four to six men. Five men are left in the man-to-man pass defense.

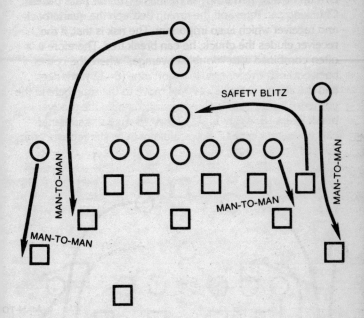

Figure 51. The safety blitz. The strong safety moves up to a position where he can blitz just before the ball is snapped. The linebacker covers the tight end man-to-man, when the safety has blitzed. The corner backs cover the wide receivers man-to-man.

A rule change in recent years has had an effect on the theory of pass defense. The receiver may only be "jammed" or "chucked" once on each play and then only within 5 yards of the line of scrimmage. This has both made it easier for receivers to get downfield and opened up the passing game. It has also made speed in the defensive backfield more important than strength. Strong backs who can bottle receivers up at the line are no longer as valuable.

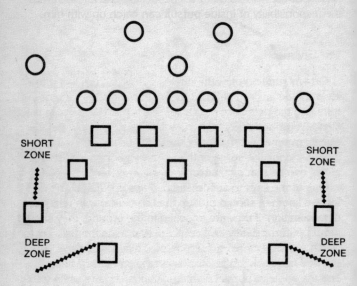

Figure 52. Double coverage on both wide receivers is indicated as both the strong safety and the free safety take the deep zones while the corner backs stay in the short zones.

Run Defense

To defend against the run, each member of the team is given a specific area of the field to protect on each play. As a running play develops, each reacts to defend his area, a "lane" that the offense could choose to attack, staying in this lane while charging the ball carrier. For example, on the pitch sweep or any wide play, the defensive backs protect the outside lane and attempt to turn the ball carrier back into the middle of the field so that the linebackers and linemen with the responsibility of inside pursuit can catch up with him.

The Linemen

On any running play, the offensive linemen are trying to clear the defensive line from the point of attack and penetrate into the defensive backfield. The job of the defense is to stand its ground and block the path of the runner. A defensive lineman who can't make the play himself can still do his job if he stops the surge of the offensive blocker so that the tackle can be made by a teammate who is free.

One of the keys to successful defense is pursuit. The defensive linemen should pursue the ball carrier with relentless determination. If they are knocked to the ground, they should jump up immediately and continue to pursue the ball. Try to watch a good defensive lineman over a series of plays. Study the way he reacts to the blocker on the line of scrimmage and the angle of pursuit as he maintains his lane while stalking the ball carrier.

The Linebackers

The linebackers are the members of the defensive unit who attempt to "search and destroy" the opponent. While the linemen in front of them bottle up a play, they come in and make the tackle. On most teams, the middle linebacker is the team leader in tackles. The linebackers pursue the wide play from the inside so that if the ball carrier cuts back they are there to greet him. They attempt to meet plays up the middle head-on and also stop the inside and off-tackle plays. Because their positioning and speed allows them to be more mobile than the linemen, on running plays they will usually be somewhere around the ball carrier. Like the linemen in front, they should be relentless in their pursuit of the ball.

The Defensive Backs

Although primarily concerned with pass defense, the defensive backs have the responsibility of containing the run. The backs are expected to be in position to make the tackle if the runner eludes the linemen or linebackers. They also must be active on the wide play and either make the tackle or force the play inside. Defensive backs must also be careful not to overreact to running plays because that will leave them vulnerable to long gains from play action passes and option plays. By watching the reaction of the defensive players to sweeps, you can see the total picture of the defense working as a unit to stop a run.

Stunting on Defense

Defensive linemen "stunt" when they vary the type and direction of their charge from one play to another. Instead of staying in the same lane play after play, the linemen line up in one area but then charge to another in a coordinated effort to disrupt the offensive blocking. A defensive end who usually rushes wide might make his move to the inside of the defensive tackle instead. Such plays can cause a mismatch by creating situations where two lineman are rushing in an area with only one blocker. In some cases, the player might take his stance as much as a yard back from the line of scrimmage so that he can "read" the blocking of the offensive linemen and react accordingly. A stunt can backfire if the offense anticipates it properly and calls a play which exploits the vacated area.

The Defense as a Weapon

One of the curiosities of football is that there are more ways to score on defense then on offense. There are only three ways to score on offense: a pass, a run, or a field goal. On defense, however, a team can score on an intercepted pass, a recovered fumble, a blocked punt, a safety (scored by tackling the opposing ball carrier in his own end zone), or a punt return. It is not unusual for a defense to account for one or two touchdowns a game. The defense is also instrumental in getting the ball in good scoring position for its offense by taking the ball away from the other team or simply by forcing the opponent to punt.

One of the tremendous advantages of the defense is that every player is allowed to be in motion at any time. This gives them extra time to adjust to offensive changes and also gives them a chance to shift their defense after the offensive play is set.

Special Defenses

As mentioned, the 3−4 and the 4−3 (with four defensive backs) are the standard defenses which you will see most of the time. In certain situations, however, teams may use different alignments. They may shift to a 5−2, or a 3−3−5, or even a 4−1−6 (four linemen, one linebacker, and six defensive backs). In short yardage situations, when the defense is convinced the offense will run the ball (third down and less then a yard to go for the first down, for example), teams will use an eight-man line, with all the linebackers lining up in the gaps between the offensive players. The three defensive backs play man-to-man defense in the unlikely event of a pass. This defense is called the *goal line defense*, because it is most often used when a defense is backed up within its 10-yard line. In such a position, every yard is critical and, because of the gravity of its situation, the defense is no longer risking giving away a long pass.

THE KICKING GAME

The kicking game requires players, lumped under the category of "special teams," to perform specific functions on kickoffs, placekicks, and punts. Each team must have platoons trained to both cover and receive kickoffs and punts and to execute or defend against the placekick. In a closely matched game, the play of the special teams can make the difference.

THE KICKOFF

The kickoff is the first play of every game. A kickoff begins each half and follows every score. For one team it is an opportunity to pin the opponent deep in their territory, for the other a chance to run the ball back into good field position.

The Kickoff as a Defensive Play

The best kickoffs are high and deep. The deeper the kick, the farther the returner has to run. The higher the kick, the more time the kicker's teammates have to run under the ball and prepare to tackle the returner. On a high kick into the end zone, the kickoff returner will not even attempt a return if the covering team is on top of him and threatens to tackle him in the end zone or close to the goal line.

The most important tactics which the kickoff-covering team should employ are the following:

1. Players on the kickoff team should sprint down the field in lanes so that they can cover the entire field. Once the

ball is fielded, they should converge on the ball carrier from their lanes. (*See Figure 53.*) It is important that they take evasive action in order to avoid blockers and stay on their feet. A player who is blocked should jump up immediately and continue to protect his lane.

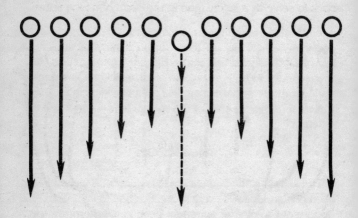

Figure 53. The kickoff-covering team maintaining position in the lanes.

2. The end players on the kickoff-covering team (designated as I and II in *Figure 54*) must not allow the ball carrier to run to the outside of them. They should turn everything toward the middle of the field, where their teammates have a chance to make the play.
3. The kicker serves as the safety man. He should not cover the kickoff at all, but should protect himself against the blockers by retreating, giving ground, and floating toward the flow of the intended return.

When watching a kickoff, check to see if it is high and deep enough to hold the ball carrier in the end zone. If the kickoff return specialist elects to attempt a return, quickly look to see if all the covering players have remained in their lanes. If they have not, look for the open areas where a long return is possible. You can also try to pick out the blocking pattern of the returning team and be aware of which players on the kickoff team have been blocked. (*See Figure 54.*) You can also quickly check the kicker to make sure he has dropped back to serve as a safety man in the event of a long return.

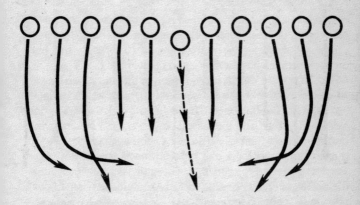

Figure 54. The kickoff-covering team identifying the blocking pattern and converging on the ball.

Basic Rules for Kickoffs

1. All players must line up even with the kicker and be behind the ball until it is kicked. If a player is ahead of the ball at the time it is kicked, he will be ruled offside, and the ball will be moved back 5 yards and kicked again.

2. If an untouched kickoff has gone out of bounds, the defensive team can take the ball where it went out of bounds or have the kicking team take a 5-yard penalty and kick again. If the ball goes out of bounds in the end

zone, it is considered a touchback and the returning team puts the ball into play at its 20-yard line.
3. Once the ball has travelled downfield a distance of 10 yards from the kicker's foot, it becomes a free ball. Either team can then recover the ball and put it in play from the point of recovery.

The Onside Kickoff as an Offensive Play

Because either team can recover the ball after it has traveled ten yards, the kicker will sometimes try to kick the ball on the ground just beyond the required 10 yards, so that his own teammates have a chance to recover the ball. This is called an onside kick. It is often seen at the end of a game when the team that has just scored is behind and desperately needs to get the ball back. The kicker will kick the ball to one side or the other, and the fastest players should be deployed on the side to which it is kicked. As soon as the kicker's foot makes contact with the ball, his teammates should drive forward and attempt to recover it. These players will try to get the ball as soon as possible, before the defense has had a chance to react. (*See Figure 55.*)

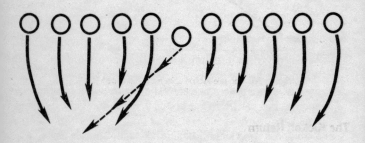

Figure 55. The onside kickoff.

In some cases, the kicking team may deploy more players on the side to which the ball will be kicked. The team lines up in the standard kickoff formation and then, just before kick, shifts extra players to the side the kicker has selected. On this play, there may be as many as nine offensive players stacked to recover the kick. (*See Figure 56.*) The trick on this play is to make the shift at the last possible minute so that the receiving team is taken by surprise.

The players on the side away from where the ball is kicked will act as safety men in the event that the receiving team fields the ball and attempts to return it. When the pre-kickoff shift is used, only one safety man is left to defend against the return.

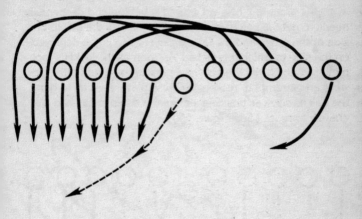

Figure 56. The pre-kickoff shift for the onside kickoff.

The Kickoff Return

The kickoff return can be one of the most dramatic plays in football. After the ball is kicked, one team charges down the field at full speed to make the tackle, while eleven opposing players travel up the field to smash a hole in the coverage. Try to identify the blocking pattern of the defense as soon as possible by watching the wedge. (*See Figure 57.*) The wedge is formed by the four players (designated as E, E, B, B in the diagram) and they will take the routes indicated in order to get into position as soon as possible to form a blocking wall for the ball carrier. The wedge will be formed approximately 10 yards in front of the point where the ball is caught, and the players in the wedge will attempt to stay in front of the ball carrier as long as possible. The return specialist who fields the kickoff (designated R1) will follow them upfield as long as he possibly can, while the other return man (designated R2) will act as a personal blocker, lead the man into the wedge, and block the first person to penetrate the wedge and threaten the ball carrier.

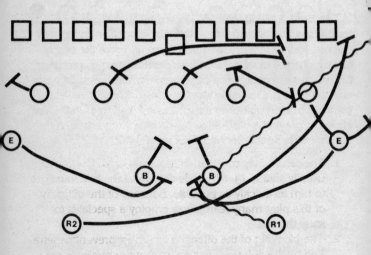

Figure 57. Following the wedge on the kickoff return.

While you are watching the wedge, look at the lead player of the kicking team as he tries to break the wedge. Leading his team, he will sprint downfield at top speed and hurl himself at the four players protecting the runner in an attempt to break open an area for his teammates to penetrate. As you can imagine, it takes a special brand of special teams player to perform this task.

The runner will be looking for an opening in the coverage, a chance to break away from the his convoy of blockers into the open field. Usually this opening will be found to the outside. Once he has made the decision to leave the wedge, he is on his own, matching his quickness and speed against that of the pursuing tacklers. Some of the most exciting running moves in football are demonstrated by kickoff return specialists after they have broken away from the wedge.

THE PUNT

The *punt,* a long high kick, is used by the offense as a fourth down play when it feels it is not in position to try for a score. Rather than try for a first down and give the other team a chance to take the ball over at the line of scrimmage, the offense will punt to the other team. When executed properly, the punt is a valuable way for a team to improve field position, but it requires an intricate combination of individual efforts to prevent a blocked kick or a long punt return. A number of factors enter into a successful punt:

1. The center snap must be accurate and hard. The punter usually stands 14–15 yards deep, and the ball must get to him as quickly as possible. Because of the difficulty of this play, many teams now employ a specialist to snap the ball.
2. The blocking of the offensive line must prevent penetration by the defensive players so that the punter is not hurried or distracted. (*See Figure 58.*)

3. The safety valve blocker, who lines up 6 yards deep, must block the first defensive man to penetrate the line and threaten the punter.
4. The punter must handle the snap cleanly and kick the ball away in 2.2 seconds. The ball must be kicked high enough to allow the players covering the punt sufficient time to get down the field. A good *hang time* (time the ball is in the air) is 4.0 to 4.5 seconds. A low punt, with low hang time, is dangerous because the ball gets to the punt returner before the coverage, and it may be returned for long yardage.
5. The linemen must quickly get down the field cover the punt. Each lineman must stay in his lane. The ends must contain the punt returner and cover from the outside. As with the kickoff, the punter stays back as a safety in case the returner breaks free.

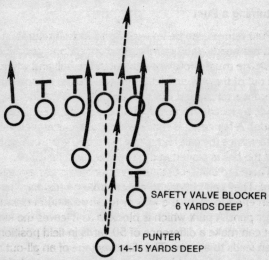

SAFETY VALVE BLOCKER
6 YARDS DEEP

PUNTER
14–15 YARDS DEEP

Figure 58. Punt protection and coverage. The players protecting the punter must block in a certain zone and not be lured from that area by a defensive stunt. The ends must protect the outside on the punt coverage and not let the punt returner outside of them.

Unlike the kickoff, a punt that goes out of bounds is dead at that point, and it does not have to be kicked over. The defense must take over that ball at that spot. When the end zone is within a punter's range, it is not unusual to see him actually try to put the ball out of bounds, angling his "coffin corner" kick so that instead of going into the end zone for a touchback it will go out of bounds between the goal line and the 20-yard line.

Another difference between a punt and a kickoff is that on a punt, the ball is not "live" after traveling 10 yards. Even if the kicking team gets to the ball before the returning team, they cannot get possession. If they touch the ball, it is considered "downed" at that spot, and the receiving team takes over. (The kicking team can recover the ball if it is first touched by the receiving team and then fumbled.)

Returning a Punt

Punt returns can be as exciting as kickoff returns. A punt returner needs good hands, good speed, and good judgement. He must know when to catch the ball and when to get out of the way and let it bounce. He must know when to attempt a return and when to call for a *fair catch* (a signal made by raising his arm high in the air before the catch is made). A fair catch is made when the receiver feels he cannot advance the ball. He cannot be hit by the onrushing tacklers and the ball is placed at the spot the catch is made.

There are different strategies a team can use against the punt. They can choose to concentrate on rushing the punter in an effort to block the kick or to cause a hurried and inferior punt. A punt which is blocked as it leaves the kicker's foot can make a difference of 50 yards in field position and often leads to a score. The disadvantage of an all-out rush is that it means fewer blockers are left to form a wedge on the return, and if the punt is not blocked, it is less likely to be returned for a big gain. The alternative strategy is to keep those players back from the line of scrimmage and set up a blocking wall for the return man.

THE FIELD GOAL AND THE EXTRA POINT

Placekicking, like punting, can appear automatic, but like the punt, the successful field goal or extra point is a result of teamwork in performing a number of separate actions. (*See Figure 59.*) Some of the essentials are the same as those for the punt: the center snap, which must be hard and true, and the blocking of the offensive line, which must keep out the defense.

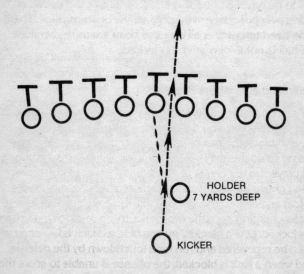

Figure 59. Field goal and extra point protection and coverage. Adequate protection depends on zone blocking. No coverage is necessary for the extra point—only for the field goal.

However the coordination of the center, holder, and kicker are the key factors for a successful kick. The center must snap the ball to the holder, the holder must catch it and put it down on a particular spot on the ground in an upright position, and the kicker must kick the ball—all in no more than 1.4 seconds. The kicker will be trying to get the ball up in the air quickly so that it won't be blocked, and at the same time musst kick it accurately enough to go over the cross bar and between the uprights. To give time for this, the blockers form a "pocket" similar to the protection formed on a drop back pass.

A field goal attempt which falls short of the back of the end zone can be returned just like a punt, so the offensive linemen must cover downfield. Nevertheless, it is rare for such a ball to be returned because the defense has the option of taking over possesion at the original line of scrimmage. There is no need to cover at all on extra point attempts, because the ball is not in play after it is kicked.

Defending against the Placekick

As soon as the ball is snapped the defensive line will do its best to break through the pocket, get their hands high in the air, and block the ball before it gets past the line of scrimmage. To do this they will put their biggest, tallest, and strongest players in the center of the defense. A wall of huge men rising above the line of scrimmage can put pressure on the holder and kicker. The defense will also have quick defensive backs charging from the two flanks, trying to block the ball as it is kicked. Like a blocked punt, a blocked kick is live and can often be recovered and run for a touchdown by the defense. And when a kick is blocked, the offense is unable to score the field goal or extra point being attempted. On both punting and placekicking plays, the charging defense must avoid running into the kicker—if the defensive player hits the kicker it is considered "roughing" and results in a 5-yard penalty and an automatic first down. (It is *not* roughing if the defense has been able to block the ball as well.)

The Two Point Play

The two-point-play-after-a-touchdown rule has added an exciting dimension to the game of college football. (It is not used by the National Football League, but it is allowed by the United States Football League.) After scoring a touchdown, the ball is placed 2 yards from the goal line, and the team which scored is given one play. If they placekick the ball and score, they are awarded one point. But they may choose to run or pass the ball over the goal line, and if they score they will be awarded two points. (In the NFL, the ball can be run or passed over the goal line but it counts as only one point.)

The opportunity to gamble for two points has resulted in another game within the game of football. The points gained or lost on two-point conversions can win or lose a game. This has dictated the development of new offensive and defensive strategy for the conversion play. One of the most effective scoring plays is the sprint-out pass, which becomes the run or pass option in this situation. The short distance required for a score forces the defense into a man-to-man defense against the pass option and presents some very exciting match-ups bewtween the wide receiver and the defensive back and between the linebacker and the running back.

WATCHING A GAME

The ideal way to watch a football game is to try to anticipate what is going to happen on each play. In order to do
this, you should always be aware of the situation before the
ball is snapped. Note the yardline, the down, and the distance
to the first-down markers. This will give you an idea of what
play will be called. For example, on second or third down and
long yardage (second and ten, or third and eight), look for
the team to pass. In short yardage situations (second and
two, third and one), you can expect a run.

When the team lines up, check the formation. Is it a pro I,
the pro set, split backs? Is the quarterback standing deep in
the backfield, in the shotgun? If so, you can expect a pass.
Has the team sent a man-in-motion? You should begin to
connect the formation with the play which follows, because
many teams use favorite formations to run certain plays.
When they set up in formation, you'll notice that detecting
the patterns on the ballfield is a lot harder then looking at
them on a diagram. But soon they will become familiar and
you'll begin to recognize the defensive setup as well.

When the ball is snapped, do not try to see everything, or
you will see nothing. If you expect a pass play, you can choose
to follow the key receivers and the patterns they are running,
or you can train your attention on the line of scrimmage and
watch the struggle of offensive linemen to keep the defensive
linemen away from the quarterback. On sweeps and traps,
keep track of the blocking of the guards. Take time during
the game to concentrate on some of the outstanding individ-
uals on the field: watch them closely during an entire series

of plays. It can be particularly rewarding to watch the match-up between an offensive lineman and his defensive counter-part for an entire series of plays.

Football is a game of situations. Every set of downs begins with first down and ten yards to go, but what happens on the first down play has a great affect on the second and third down. If a run went for 7 yards, the defense must steel itself to protect against a short yardage play. The offense is in con-trol; they can run for the 3 yards or they can call a play action pass, faking a run up the middle and looking for a long pass against a shortened-up defense.

On the other hand, if a first down pass falls incomplete, then the defense can drop back a bit, play a bit looser against the run, and protect against the medium and long pass routes. If a second down pass is also incomplete, then the defense might take out a linebacker and add another defen-sive back to strengthen their zone defense. The situation can extend or limit the options of the offense.

As the game progresses, the play will begin to be affected by the score. A team that is behind will feel pressure to catch up and will be more likely to gamble with a trick play or a long pass or, if they score, an onside kick. The team with the lead might start to play more cautiously, calling only short passes and conservative running plays to minimize the risk of turnovers.

A game also becomes affected by its own history. We have talked about the adjustments that get made over the course of a game. What happens in the first quarter can affect what happens in the fourth. If a cornerback gets beaten on a long pass, you can bet the receiver will be able to pick up good yardage on a curl pattern. A certain move early in the day might fool a linebacker once, but when it is tried again in the fourth quarter, he might be looking for it and the same play could be thrown for a loss. As you watch the game, keep track of the tendencies of each team. Do they ever throw a fly pattern on second and short? Are they running every time on first down? Is the pattern of their play calling predictable? Do they ever run when there are four receivers in the game? Note which plays have been effective, and try to detect the changes the defense makes to compensate.

As you watch the game, you can train yourself to measure a team's effectiveness by more than yards gained or lost. If a quarterback is having trouble completing passes, try to figure out the source of his problem. Is he being forced to hurry his throws because of pressure from the defensive line? Are his passes being dropped by his receivers? Is the coverage too tight? Is he trying too many long passes and not enough high-percentage, short completions? If he is intercepted, is it because he threw the ball badly or because the football tipped off the hands of a receiver? Once you understand what each player is trying to do, you will find it easier to measure his performance.

As a viewer, it is fun to match wits with the coaches and quarterbacks, and you can share in the challenge of anticipating and then reading a play as it unfolds. Remember, though, that these ballplayers not only have to recognize the plays in a split second but that in that same time they have to get their bodies in motion to react to the play. It's much easier to notice a player open in the seam of a zone then to hit him in the hands with a football.

As you know, there is a big difference between watching a game on television and seeing one in a stadium. On television, your attention is focused for you and details are rerun on videotape. The camera concentrates on the ball. It rarely provides the viewer a chance to follow pass routes and coverages and other detailed action away from the backfield before the ball is thrown. At a live event you have the freedom to study whichever facet of a play you choose. The drawback is that you must provide the concentration and analysis yourself—but with this knowlege in hand, that should be no problem at all.